**DVD and Lesson Book**

DVD Jazz Guitar

Written by Joe Charupakorn, Kurt Plahna, Chad Johnson & Michael Mueller
Video Performers: Wolf Marshall & Tom Kolb

ISBN: 978-1-4234-6224-8

7777 W. BLUEMOUND RD. P.O. BOX 13819 MILWAUKEE, WI 53213

Visit Hal Leonard Online at
www.halleonard.com

Table of Contents

Introduction

Welcome to *Jazz Guitar*, from Hal Leonard's exciting new At a Glance series. Not as formal and slow-moving as traditional method books, the material in *Jazz Guitar* is presented in a snappy and fun manner intended to have you playing over changes in virtually no time at all. Plus, the At a Glance series uses real phrases and licks by real artists to illustrate how the concepts you're learning are applied over standards and bop songs. For example, in *Jazz Guitar*, you'll get to check out Pat Martino's fiery chromatic licks on "Oleo," Pat Metheny's modern triad excursions on "Solar," and Jim Hall's refined elegance on "St. Thomas," to name just a few.

Additionally, each book in the At a Glance series comes with a DVD containing video lessons that correspond to the printed material. The DVD that accompanies this book contains four video lessons, each approximately 8 to 10 minutes in length, that correspond to the topics covered in *Jazz Guitar*. In these videos, ace instructors Wolf Marshall and Tom Kolb will show you in great detail everything from substitute chords in a jazz blues, to playing hip, "outside" lines. As you go through *Jazz Guitar*, try to play the examples first on your own, and then check out the DVD for additional help or to see if you played them correctly. As the saying goes, "A picture is worth a thousand words," so be sure to use this invaluable tool on your quest to becoming a jazz guitarist.

If you're a rock or blues guitar player and you've been curious about the mysterious realm of jazz, then you've come to the right place. We're going to get your feet wet with some basic jazz rhythm and harmony concepts that will open the door to the huge world of jazz guitar.

BEGINNING JAZZ RHYTHM GUITAR

Seventh Chords

Jazz harmony is steeped in the use of seventh chords, which are made up of the root, 3rd, 5th, and 7th degrees of a scale. You'll rarely hear chords smaller than a seventh chord used when a jazzer plays over standards, although sometimes triads may be used to evoke a "classical" sound. The rule of thumb however, is that you want to play at least a seventh chord (if not a more extended chord like a 9th, 11th, or 13th) in most situations, if nothing else, to be stylistically appropriate so as to avoid the "evil eye" from people you're playing with. Think of it like this: if you were running for President of the United States, would you do your interviews wearing a Van Halen T-shirt?

You'll want to become familiar with all of the common seventh-chord voicings used in jazz, which are a bit different than the open or barre chord voicings that you might be used to. Luckily, the shapes you'll learn are moveable, just like the barre chords, so after you learn one new shape, you've actually learned twelve chords!

To keep this lesson uniform and systematic, we'll only focus on movable four-note shapes in root position and first, second, and third inversions. None of the chord tones in the voicings will be doubled or missing.

We'll also only play voicings with bass notes on the 6th string and in doing so, we'll always keep the 5th string muted. Of course, you'll eventually want to explore the infinite amount of chord voicings and string combinations that are possible on the fretboard, but for now, this is a good place to start.

Major Seventh Chord: 1–3–5–7

The first type of chord we'll study is the major seventh chord, which contains the 1st, 3rd, 5th, and 7th degrees of the major scale. As a general rule, these four notes can be arranged in any order as long as each note is present and accounted for. This rule applies to the other types of seventh chords you'll learn as well.

We'll play all our chords in the key of F for example purposes, but you should learn them in all 12 keys. Major seventh chords have a "happy" sound, although the seventh does add a nice little "rub" to it that gives it more of an edge than a major triad. Nonetheless, the major seventh chord sounds pretty resolved and is often used as the tonic (I) chord.

Fmaj7—Root Position

Here's the root position voicing of Fmaj7. In this voicing the notes from bottom to top are F–E–A–C.

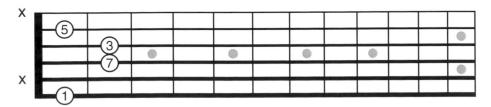

Mute or damp the 5th string with your left-hand index finger to keep the open string from ringing.

Although some "guitar authorities" may say this is a guitar technique no-no, you can also finger this chord using your thumb if you'd like. The very real advantage to using the thumb on some bass notes is that it keeps other fingers free to use for embellishments, chord extensions, or chord melodies. If you use your thumb for the Fmaj7 here, you can also use it to mute the 5th string while you're at it.

Fmaj7—First Inversion

Here's Fmaj7 in first inversion. First inversion means that the 3rd of the chord, A in this case, is in the bass instead of the root, F, which is located on the fourth string.

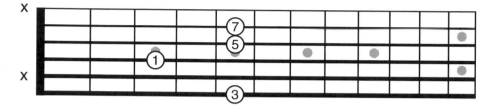

These are the same notes as before, but they've been re-configured from bottom to top as A–F–C–E.

Fmaj7—Second Inversion

Now we have the second inversion, with the 5th, C, in the bass. This voicing has a colorful half-step clash on top between the 7th and the root, which is played on the second string.

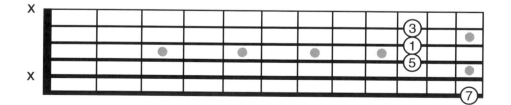

Fmaj7—Third Inversion

And finally, we have the third inversion of Fmaj7, with the 7th, E, in the bass. The root is located on the third string. Note that this voicing isn't used as much as the others because of the dissonance from the bottom E note to F (it's a gnarly ♭9!), but it's still good to know and understand.

Dominant Seventh Chord: 1–3–5–♭7

The dominant seventh chord contains the same notes as the major seventh chord, except one note is changed; the 7th is lowered by a half step. This gives the chord a funky, bluesy sound.

We'll play all the chords in F again. You'll notice that compared to the major seventh chords you just learned, only that one tone—the 7th—is changed throughout all of the voicings. The root of each chord and inversion will be on the same string it was on for the F major seventh chords and inversions.

F7—Root Position

This is F7 in root position.

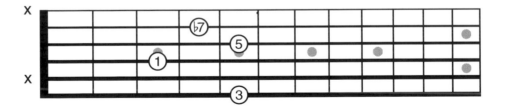

Again, you can use your thumb on this one or barre strings 4 and 2 with your index finger. Now you have two fingers that aren't occupied.

F7—First Inversion

Here's the first inversion. This one might be tough to grab. Finger this one using the ring finger on the sixth string, index finger on the fourth string, pinky on the third string, and middle finger on the second string.

F7—Second Inversion

Second inversion. This shape is similar to the open-position C7 chord, just with the middle finger on the sixth string rather than the fifth string.

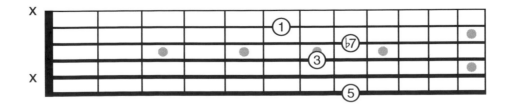

6

F7—Third Inversion

And third inversion. This is a pretty easy shape; just barre the fourth, third, and second strings with your index finger and use your middle finger for the note on the sixth string.

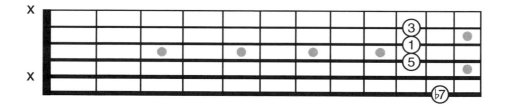

Minor Seventh Chord: 1–♭3–5–♭7

Next, we have minor seventh chords. To create a minor seventh chord, take a dominant 7th chord and lower the 3rd. Now, the overall tonality is minor, although it doesn't sound quite as sad as a minor triad. Again, in all the voicings of the minor seventh chord that you'll learn here, the root is on the same strings as the previous F major and dominant seventh chords and inversions.

Fm7—Root Position

Here's Fm7 in root position. You can again use the thumb to fret the bass note and index finger to barre the rest; another common fingering is to grab the bass note with the middle finger and barre the rest with the ring finger.

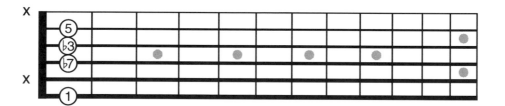

Fm7—First Inversion

Here's the first inversion.

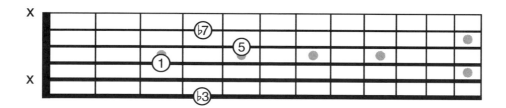

Fm7—Second Inversion

The second inversion. You can use a barre to catch the notes on the fourth and second strings.

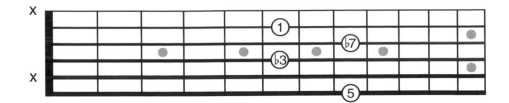

Fm7—Third Inversion

Third inversion. If you ignore the bass note, this shape may look familiar—it looks like an open-position A minor chord shape. Just play that shape and add the pinky for the bass note.

ii–V–I PROGRESSION

Now that we've got the fundamental chord voicings under our belt, it's time to put them to use. The most common chord progression heard in jazz is the ii–V–I. You've probably heard it used in other kinds of music as well, since the progression has a built-in sense of tension and release—the tension of the ii and V resolving back to home base, or the I chord.

Let's apply our chord voicings to the ii–V–I. Now, one of the conveniences of knowing all the inversions of the chords is that we can play several different chords in one position without jumping around the neck. This will make changing chords easier.

As you learn these chords, pay attention to where the chord tones are located in each voicing, and how each tone moves as you change chords. This is called *voice leading*. The idea is to have each note of the chord either remain stationary or move smoothly to the tones in the next chord by only half or whole steps, rather than leaps or skips. Doing this will create a sort of sub-melody, which is really the essence of harmony. If you develop an interest in studying voice leading, you may want to check out the four-part chorales by J.S. Bach. While the Bach Chorales fall under the classical category, rather than jazz, they provide an invaluable study in perfect voice leading by one of history's musical masters. With these concepts internalized, making the transition into jazz harmony should be pretty straightforward. The sooner you can wrap your head around these concepts, the more you will understand jazz, (and all music, for that matter).

Here is a ii–V–I in the key of F. The ii is Gm7, the V is C7, and the I is Fmaj7. By playing the ii and I chords as root position chords and the V as a second inversion, all the chords lay out nicely in this one area of the neck. Check out the careful voice leading between these three chords. From Gm7 to C7, the notes on the sixth and third strings stay the same, while the notes on the fourth and second strings move down by step. From C7 to Fmaj7, the notes on the fourth and second strings stay the same, and the notes on the sixth and third strings move down by step.

Now let's try the same thing with a different combination of inversions. Here we have a first-inversion ii chord going to a third-inversion V chord to a first-inversion I chord. Again, study the voice leading—although it may seem subtle, it's actually a very important concept that you should always keep in mind.

Here's another combination with that hip third-inversion major 7 voicing that contains the half step on top.

Rhythm Changes

"Rhythm changes" is a very common jazz progression based on George Gershwin's "I Got Rhythm." You'll find rhythm changes throughout the jazz idiom, particularly in bebop, where must-know tunes like "Anthropology" and "Oleo" (both based on rhythm changes) are ubiquitous.

For instance, here's Pat Martino's take on "Oleo."

"OLEO"
Pat Martino

By Sonny Rollins

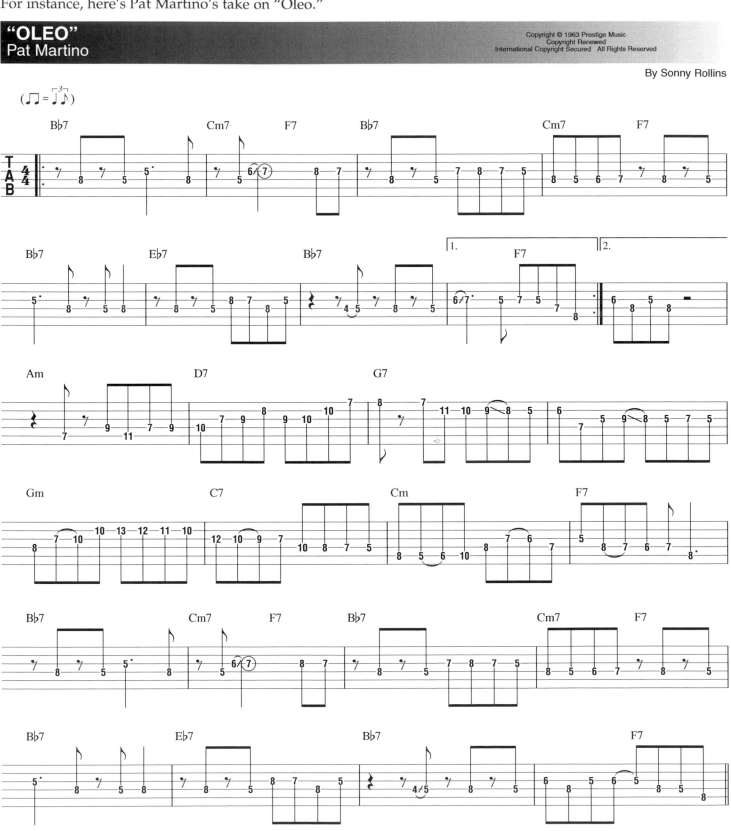

Generally speaking, all rhythm changes songs are thirty two-measures long and written with an AABA form.

The A section consists of this progression (countless variations exist), played as two chords per measure:

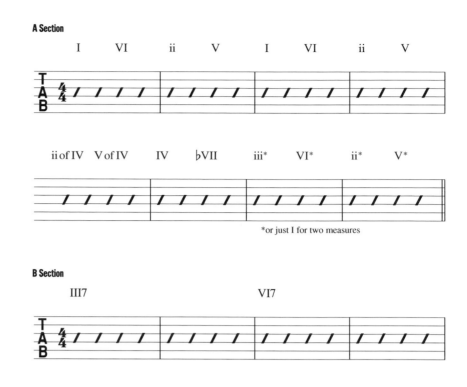

A Section

| I | VI | ii | V | I | VI | ii | V |

| ii of IV | V of IV | IV | ♭VII | iii* | VI* | ii* | V* |

*or just I for two measures

The B section begins on the III7 chord and continues up a cycle of fourths with each chord lasting for two measures apiece:

B Section

| III7 | | VI7 | |

| II7 | | V7 | |

So, in the key of B♭ the basic progression is:

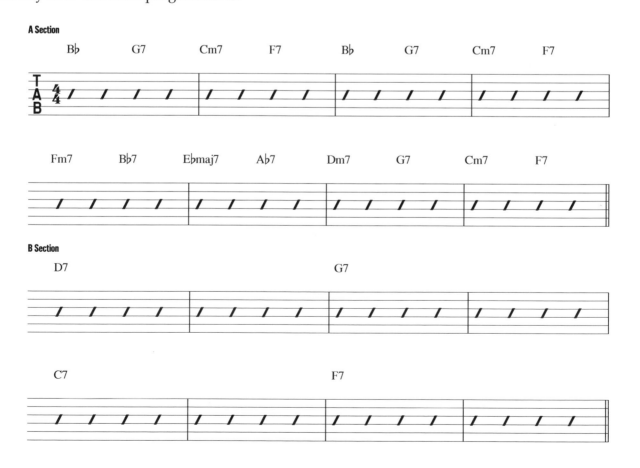

A Section

| B♭ | G7 | Cm7 | F7 | B♭ | G7 | Cm7 | F7 |

| Fm7 | B♭7 | E♭maj7 | A♭7 | Dm7 | G7 | Cm7 | F7 |

B Section

| D7 | | G7 | |

| C7 | | F7 | |

In this example, watch how the chosen inversions work out in the same areas of the neck with minimal jumping around. Again, study the voice leading from chord to chord.

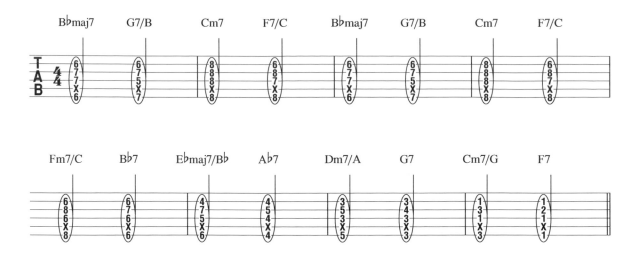

You should play the rhythm changes progression in all keys—it's a great exercise for learning how to play and hear chord changes fluently. It will also thoroughly prepare you for many progressions you'll encounter in other jazz tunes. Try different combinations of inversions as well. Note that in addition to this version, there are countless variations of the rhythm changes progression with substitute chords. You will almost certainly encounter some of these variations in your future jazz travels.

Freddie Green Comping Style

Now that you have some chords and progressions together, let's talk briefly about comping, which is jazz lingo for "accompanying," or playing chords behind a melody or soloist. There are as many different ways to comp as there are people in the world, but one of the most common styles was established by jazz guitarist Freddie Green.

Now, Freddie Green didn't necessarily invent this style all on his own, but he was known for it, and certainly many a jazzer has thoroughly ingested his simple, yet ingenious comping style.

Freddie's style involves strumming chords in quarter notes on every beat of the measure. Go for a somewhat percussive attack. You can also try making the chord stabs on beats 1 and 3 longer and the ones on beats 2 and 4 shorter. This style is also useful if you're playing in a duo, without a rhythm section. Hitting the chords on all the beats keeps the time lucid for the soloist.

For these examples, we're going to use three-note voicings, leaving out the note on the B string. This thinning out of voicings is very common in the Freddie Green style.

Let's try this with a ii–V–I in B♭. Note that in measure 4, a G7 is added to further push into the Cm7. This G7 functions as a *secondary dominant*, which is a dominant chord that doesn't occur naturally in the key. Secondary dominants are used to create the dominant-tonic sense of urgency to a chord other than the tonic chord.

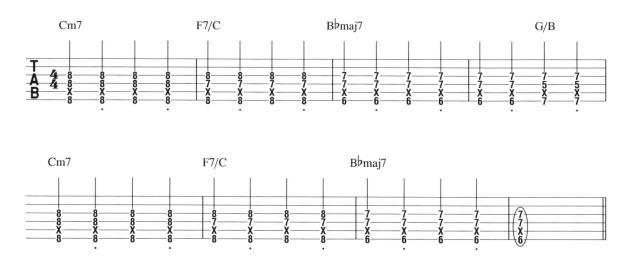

Now let's apply this comping style to the rhythm changes that you've become acquainted with.

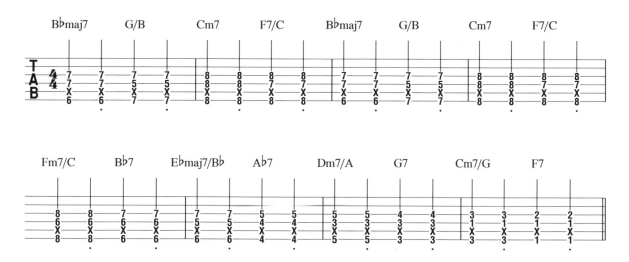

Now that you've got some of the basics down, let's explore some jazz blues progressions.

JAZZ BLUES PROGRESSIONS

Jazz and blues have been intertwined since the beginning, and the 12-bar form has been the basis for countless standards. In fact, many of the most regarded bebop standards like saxophonist Charlie Parker's "Au Privave" and pianist Thelonius Monk's "Straight, No Chaser" are simply 12-bar blues, albeit with jazz changes.

As a jazz guitarist, it's just about mandatory that you can fluently navigate the 12-bar blues. Virtually every major jazz guitarist (Wes Montgomery, George Benson, Jim Hall, Mike Stern, Pat Metheny, and John Scofield, to name the most prominent) has played and recorded the blues. At jazz jam sessions where often you end up on the bandstand with total strangers, it's almost guaranteed that at some point a blues will be played because everyone is expected to be able to play the blues.

Standard 12-bar Changes

Here are the standard blues changes in the key of C using mostly stock chord voicings. Be sure to practice this in all keys, and if these voicings are already familiar to you, be sure to practice the progression with some of the more colorful voicings you know.

The chords for a standard blues in C are:

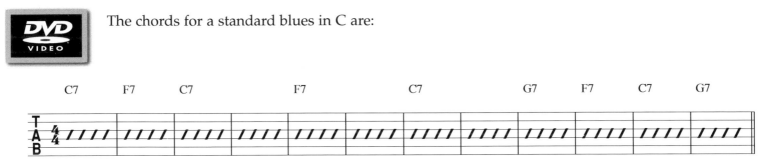

These are the basic changes used primarily by rock and blues players. You'll hear this in the music of say, Cream or B.B. King, but jazz players may sometimes use this set of changes as well.

Here's an example of B.B. King playing a blues.

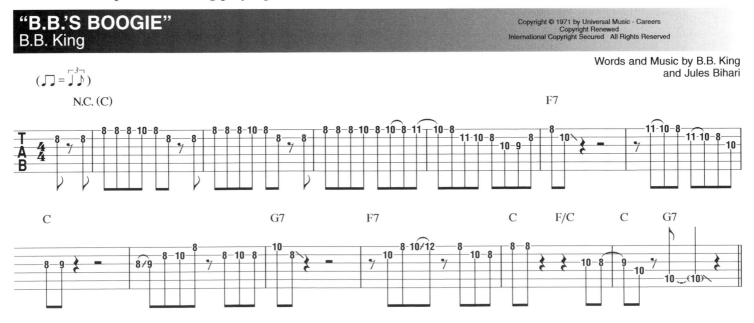

This is once through the form, which is sometimes called a "chorus" of blues. What generally happens is that after you reach the end of a chorus, you'll start the whole form over again, repeating it as many times as necessary to accommodate solos or vocals.

As you can see, we used only the I, IV, and V chords. However, there are countless variations on this progression, especially in jazz where there are literally hundreds or maybe thousands if you counted every possible chord variation. But, once you get familiar with the basic ideas involved, you'll be able to draw on all these variations at will, depending upon what the situation calls for. We'll check out some variations, getting a little more complex, step by step.

The I–VI–ii–V Turnaround

The first way we can dress this up to make it more jazzy is by changing the second half of the progression to a I–VI–ii–V. Instead of hanging on the tonic C7 for measures 7 and 8, we'll play C7 in measure 7.

C7

And then we'll play an altered A7 in measure 8. In this case, we'll use A7#9.

A7#9

This A7 here is a secondary dominant. Specifically, this A7 functions as the V of ii. Usually, the vi chord in the key of C would be Am, but we've made it a dominant chord to increase the pull to the next chord, which would be Dm7.

Dm7

That's the ii chord, which leads to the V chord, G7.

G7

After that, we repeat the I–VI–ii–V cycle, but twice as fast, and that would round out the 12 bars. Here's the new progression.

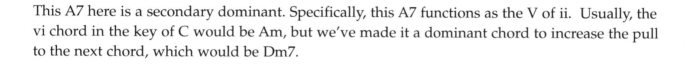

If this is confusing to you, here is a reference chart of all the naturally occurring 7th chords in a major key.

Scale Degree	7th Chord
I	maj7
ii	m7
iii	m7
IV	maj7
V	dom7
vi	m7
vii°	m7♭5

As mentioned earlier, there are hundreds of variations of the 12-bar form, and this is a good example. Sometimes you may actually see the A chord as Am7, which would be a diatonic vi chord in C (see chart above). Obviously, if you're playing with other musicians, you'll need to decide which version you'll be playing—writing out a chart can help in the beginning. Eventually though, you'll know this like the back of your hand, and it will become more instinctual.

Here's an example of Mike Stern comping through a I–VI–ii–V progression from an original blues of his called "That's What You Think." The VI chord here is labeled as D7♯9, a dominant chord with alterations. We'll cover altered chords later in the chapter (see page 19). Notice that he's only using small, two-note voicings here. These voicings are comprised of the crucial 3rd and 7th of each chord—these are the notes that define the chord's sound.

"THAT'S WHAT YOU THINK"
Mike Stern

By Mike Stern

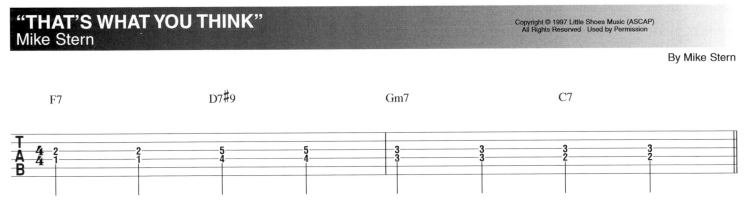

And here's Stern blowing over the I–VI–ii–V progression in that same tune. In this selection, he's whipping out the speedy long lines that he's known for.

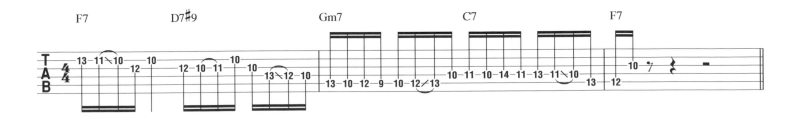

ii–V of IV

The next change we can make will be in measure 4. Instead of hanging on the I chord for measures 3 and 4, we'll temporarily *tonicize* (using a secondary dominant to create the impression of a new tonal center) the IV chord by playing a ii–V leading into it.

So, after the C7 in measure 3, we're going to play Gm7 for two beats:

Gm7

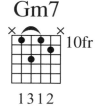

Then C7 for beats 3 and 4.

C7

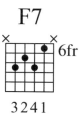

This C7 then leads us to the IV chord, F7.

F7

So, here is the progression up through measure 5.

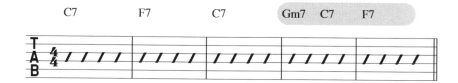

Here's the ii–V of IV as used in a standard—Duke Ellington's "In a Mellow Tone" as played by Joe Pass.

"IN A MELLOW TONE"
Joe Pass

By Duke Ellington

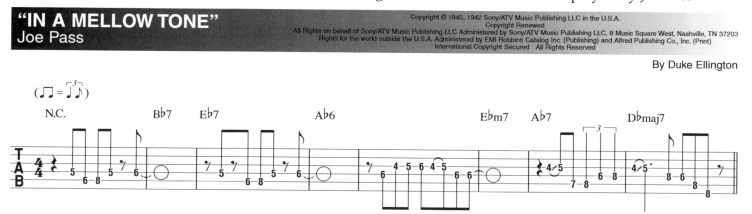

♯iv°7 Chord

We stopped there at measure 5, because another very common jazz move happens in measure 6. Instead of repeating the IV chord, F7, we'll move the bass line chromatically up and play an F♯°7 chord. This is a diminished chord, built off the ♯4 scale degree.

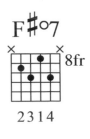

It's commonly followed with the I chord in measure 7.

Here's an example of the ♯iv°7 from "St. Thomas," as played by Jim Hall.

"ST. THOMAS"
Jim Hall

By Sonny Rollins

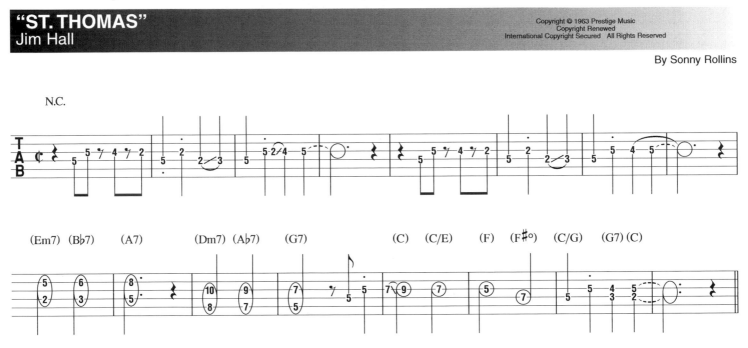

Let's take a look at the whole 12-bar progression with everything we've added to see how far we've come.

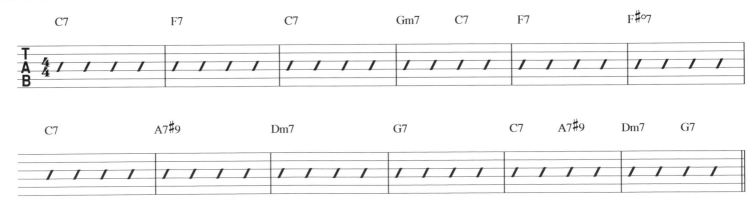

Extended Chords and Altered Dominants

Now, this is a fairly standard jazz blues, so before we complicate it any further, let's talk about a few other ways to make it jazzier.

One very common way is to replace the basic I, IV, and V chords with extended chords, like 9ths or 13ths. As long as the replacement chord has the same root and tonality (major 7, minor 7, dominant 7, etc.) you can freely interchange them. That's why, even though a jazz chart might only say things like Cm7 or C7, the guitarist might actually play a Cm11 or C9. As long as the chord still serves the same overall function, it can be used.

For example, you might use a C13 for the I chord.

And maybe you'll use an F9 for the IV chord.

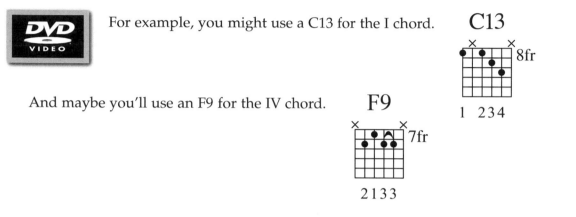

Both the C13 and the F9 sound more or less like the original C7 and F7.

Experiment with this concept. You'll find that some choices work better than others and most often, it's the context that determines the "rightness" of the chord. The fun and sometimes perplexing thing about jazz is that, while there are general guidelines, there are no hard-and-fast rules. Some extensions tend to work better than others at different points in the progression. In the end, it's all about whether it sounds good to you or not—and that could even mean something like putting a ♯9 on a major 7 chord.

Any chord type can be extended. For example, you can extend the minor chords in ii–Vs as well. Another way to sophisticate things is by using altered dominants (dominant chords that have a ♭9 or a ♯9 and/or a ♭5 or a ♯5).

Try replacing plain 7th chords with altered ones. Note, however, that this usually sounds best on the *functioning dominants*—that is, the ones that do actually lead down a 5th, or up a 4th, to the next chord, as the altered notes work in tandem with the already strong pull of a functional dominant chord.

NON-FUNCTIONING DOMINANTS

A *non-functioning dominant* chord is one that does not resolve down a 5th, or up a 4th. For example, the B♭9 in measure 4 of "Moonlight in Vermont," played by Johnny Smith, is a non-functioning dominant chord because it doesn't resolve up a 4th to E♭, as might be expected.

"MOONLIGHT IN VERMONT"
Johnny Smith

Words by John Blackburn
Music by Karl Suessdorf

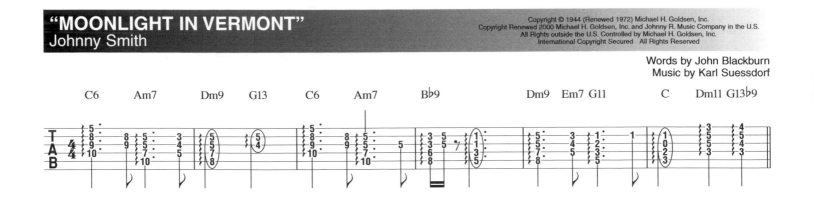

 So, you could choose to add an altered C7 chord in the ii–V of measure 4 and get something like this: Gm9.

Gm9

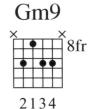

Followed by this C+7, which is sometimes called C7♯5.

And then F9.

Note that, although the extensions and alterations add a distinct dash of color, the basic function of the ii and V chords are still clear.

Here's what the progression looks and sounds like using some of these extensions and altered dominants. Remember, you have the freedom to mix and match as you like. Let good judgment be your guide. This sense is best cultivated by extensive and attentive listening to the way the masters like Wes Montgomery and Joe Pass did it.

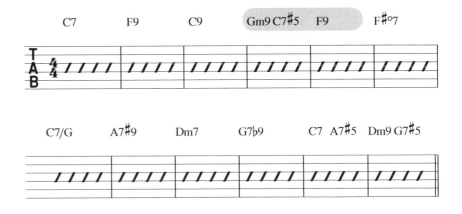

Keep in mind that these are just a few of the variations you could play on this version of a standard jazz blues. Sometimes jazz musicians can take it so far "out" that you almost wouldn't know that it's a blues they're playing; they can also play it so simply that you think you're listening to a traditional blues artist rather than a jazz master. Some of jazz guitarist Grant Green's music is like that; it sounds so simple, yet is so swinging and strong that you forego the cerebral aspect of jazz. The fun part is that, ultimately, it's entirely up to you—granted you really have the basic concepts at your disposal.

Other ii–Vs and Tritone Substitutions

Let's make the progression more complex by adding some more ii–Vs. For example, instead of just having an altered A7 in measure 8, we can play Em7♭5–A7 to create a ii–V of the ii chord, Dm7, in measure 9.

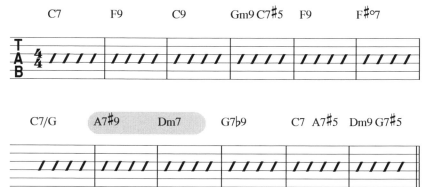

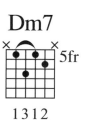

 So, in measure 7, you'd have your C7, let's say.

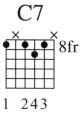

Then for measure 8, we'd have Em7♭5 to A7 altered, like this.

The Em7♭5 and A7 altered then lead to Dm7.

While we're at it, we could replace the I chord at the beginning of measure 11 with the same iii chord (Em7♭5), which would create the same ii–V of ii cycle. Since there are so many variations, you'll sometimes see the iii chord as an Em7♭5 and other times just as a standard Em7—both versions are played just as often, and are equally valid.

Here's how the progression looks now:

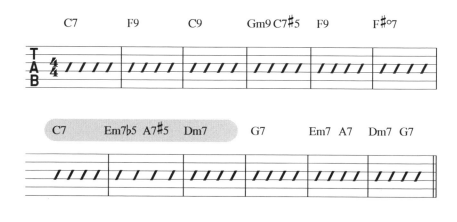

To make things even more interesting, we can use something called *tritone subs* (substitutes) during those quick ii–Vs. A tritone sub is a substitute dominant chord that's located a tritone (three whole steps) away from the original chord. The reason dominant chords a tritone apart can easily be interchanged is that both chords share the most important of common tones—the 3rd and ♭7th, the two crucial notes that define a chord's tonality. For example, the notes of an A7 chord are A, C♯, E, and G. A7's tritone sub is E♭7, and its notes are E♭, G, B♭, D♭. The C♯ (spelled enharmonically as D♭ for the E♭7 chord) functions as the 3rd of A7 and the ♭7 of E♭7, and the G conversely functions as the ♭7 of A and the 3rd of E♭7. Just these two notes played simultaneously aurally signify either A7 or E♭7.

The remaining two notes function as alterations. For example, against an A root, superimposing the notes of E♭7 produces the ♭5 (E♭) and the ♭9 (B♭). Likewise, against an E♭ root, superimposing the notes of A7 produces the same alterations, the ♭5 (A) and the ♭9 (E).

TRITONE SUBSTITUTE

A7 =	A	C♯	E	G
	Root	3rd	5th	♭7th
E♭7 =	E♭	G	B♭	D♭
	Root	3rd	5th	♭7th

E♭7/A =	E♭	G	B♭	D♭(C♯)
	♭5th	♭7th	♭9th	3rd
A7/E♭ =	A	C♯(D♭)	E	G
	♭5th	♭7th	♭9th	3rd

Tritone subs allow us to create chromatically descending bass lines. For example, instead of Em7–A7 to Dm7 in measures 8–9, we could replace the A7 with its tritone sub, E♭7, and get something like this: Em7, E♭9, and Dm9.

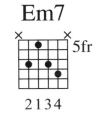

Em7

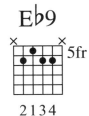

E♭9   Dm9

Here's a great example from Wes Montgomery's "Sundown," a fancy blues in A. In measure 8, he uses a ii–V of ii (C#m7–F#7b9). After arriving on the ii chord, he inserts a slick ascending progression that leads to a chromatically-descending cycle.

"SUNDOWN"
Wes Montgomery

By John L. "Wes" Montgomery

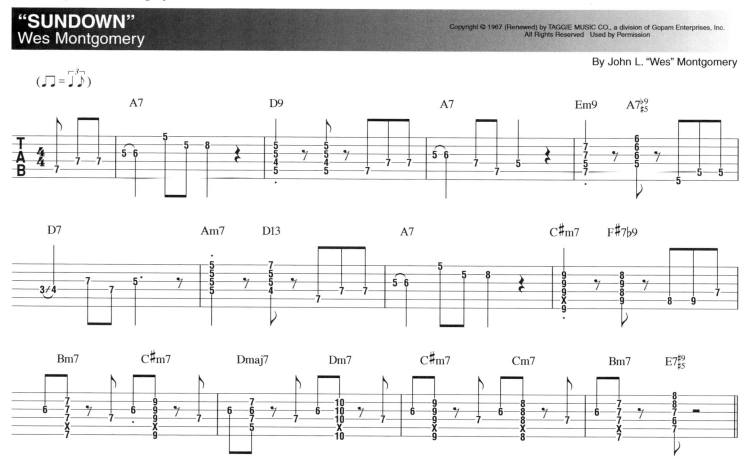

Parker Blues

Charlie Parker took these types of changes to the limit in tunes like "Blues for Alice." This alternate version of the blues subsequently came to be known as the "Parker Blues."

With a maj7 chord as the tonic, this is about as colorful as blues changes get. Here's the progression in C.

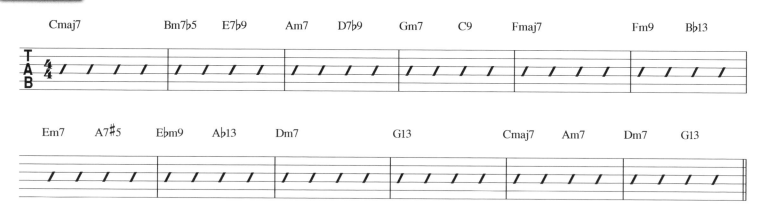

Note how the series of ii–Vs starting in measure 2 are employed directly to ultimately lead into the Fmaj7 chord in measure 5. Then, starting from measure 6, a series of chromatically-descending ii–Vs lead perfectly into the Dm7 chord in measure 9.

While this version only really resembles the blues slightly in terms of harmony, the 12-bar form and the IV chord in measure 5 still make the form recognizable. The near-infinite variations on the blues form should be enough to keep you busy for a long time, especially when you practice them in every key—which, of course, you should be doing. And no matter what type of tunes you play, be it standard, modal, or free, you can never really have jazz without the blues.

Here are some challenging blues heads for you to digest.

First, here's George Benson's take on the Charlie Parker classic, "Billie's Bounce."

"BILLIE'S BOUNCE" (BILL'S BOUNCE)
George Benson

By Charlie Parker

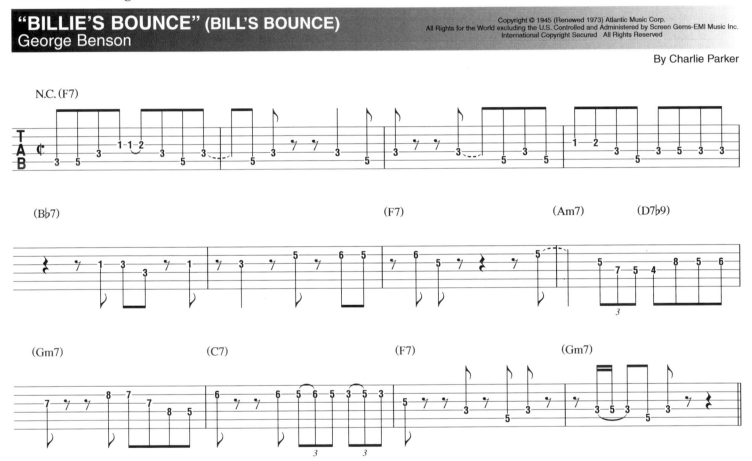

And now check out Mike Stern's original blues, "That's What You Think."

"THAT'S WHAT YOU THINK"
Mike Stern

By Mike Stern

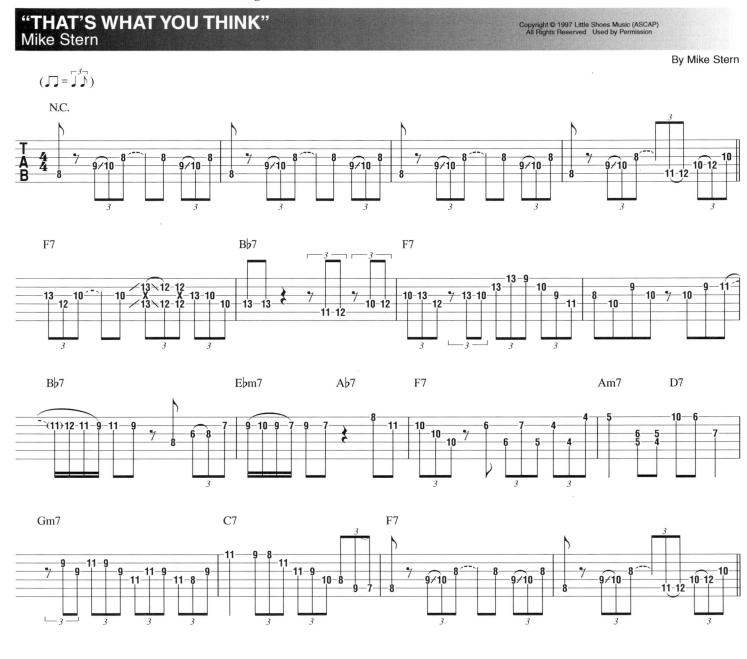

BEGINNING ii–V–I LICKS

The ii–V–I progression is the backbone of hundreds of jazz tunes—not to mention many pop songs and standards as well. It's the equivalent of the I–IV–V progression in the blues. We touched on the progression in the Beginning Jazz Progressions lesson and now we are going to create licks using that progression. Because the ii–V–I progression occurs so frequently in jazz standards, it is practically required for all jazz musicians to learn ii–V–I patterns and licks.

In case you skipped ahead and came straight for the licks, we need to make sure we know what a ii–V–I progression is. When we say "ii–V–I," we're referring to the root notes of the chords built off the second, fifth, and first degrees of a scale. In jazz, of course, these are usually seventh chords or other types of extended chords. If you're still not sure what that means, refer to the previous sections of this book.

For example, in the key of C major, a ii–V–I progression is as follows: Dm7, G7, and Cmaj7.

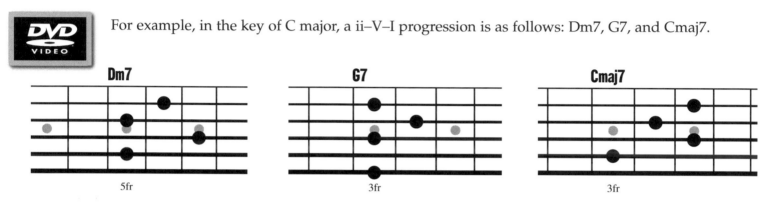

If you're not familiar with diatonic harmony in all 12 keys, you'll probably want to read up on how to harmonize a scale with triads and seventh chords; it's pretty essential knowledge for jazz improvisation.

In this lesson, we're going to work in the key of C for the sake of simplicity, but make sure you practice what you learn in all 12 twelve keys. Ok, so now that we know a ii–V–I progression, how do we come up with a lick to play over it? Well, there are a few different ways to go about it.

Scalar Approach

One method is a scalar approach. Each diatonic chord in a key has a mode associated with it. This approach relates every chord to its appropriate scale.

In the key of C, for the ii chord, Dm7, the appropriate mode is **D Dorian**.

For the V chord, G7, the matching mode would be **G Mixolydian**.

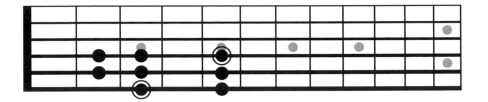

And for the I chord, Cmaj7, the mode would be **C Ionian**. This is just the same as a C major scale.

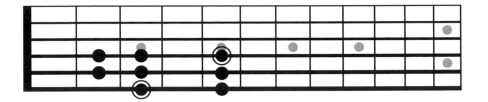

If you're familiar with the modes, then you may be aware that D Dorian, G Mixolydian, and C Ionian all share the same notes. This means that against Dm7–G7–Cmaj7, you could improvise just using the C major scale, and, for the most part, it will sound good. Of course, if you relate each chord to its mode, you'll be able to hone in closer to the sound of the specific chord. For a more detailed explanation of the modes, check out *DVD Scales & Modes*, also in the At a Glance series.

So, if we wanted to write a lick with this approach, we might come up with something like this:

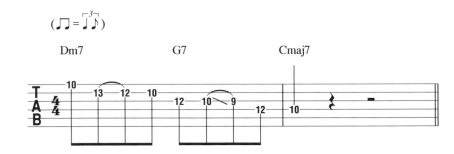

So, if you noticed in that lick, we're just descending down four notes of D Dorian, then down four notes of G Mixolydian, and then resolving to the root of C. You may also have noticed that we descended straight down a C major scale, but the notes lined up nicely against the underlying chords to create a harmonically-cogent lick. For example, on the Dm7 chord, the first note played is D, the root; over the G7 chord, the first note played is G, the root; and on the resolution to C, the note played is C, the root. Even though we're just running down the C major scale, we're still relating each chord with its appropriate mode.

In this example from Grant green's solo on "Speak Low," against a ii–V–I in F (Gm7–C7–Fmaj7), Green's lines are based on descending down the F major scale. If you look closely however, the chord changes are delineated in his lines. The first note over Gm7 is B♭, the ♭3, the first note over C7 is E, the 3rd, and on the resolution to F, the first note played is A, the 3rd.

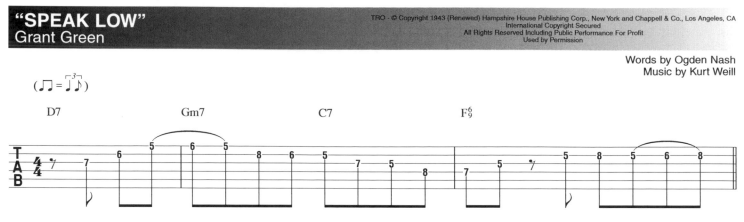

The ii–V–I occurs commonly in several forms. The length of time each chord lasts will determine how many notes you need for each chord. The previous examples we looked at have the ii and V chords lasting for two beats each and the I chord lasting a measure. Just as common is with the ii and V chords each lasting one measure and the I chord lasting for two measures. Here's an example. With the chords lasting twice as long in this one, you'll most likely play more notes for each chord.

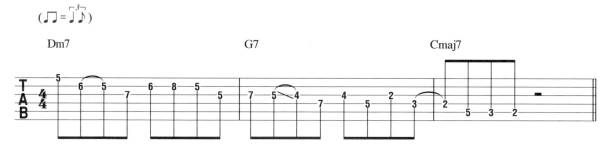

Here's what Grant Green does in the same "Speak Low" solo when the chords last twice as long. Note here that the I chord, F, is substituted with iii, Am7. This substitution is along the lines of what we discussed earlier in the Jazz Blues Progressions chapter.

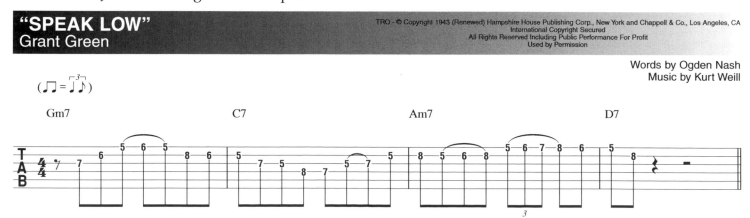

Mike Stern plays step-wise scalar lines in his solo to "Nardis."

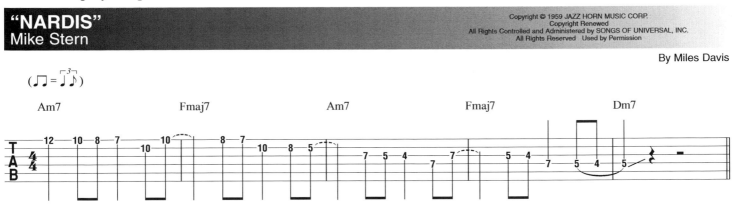

By Miles Davis

Later in Stern's "Nardis" solo, he implies a three-against-four rhythm, while taking a scalar approach. Using rhythmic devices like this is a good way to make things interesting.

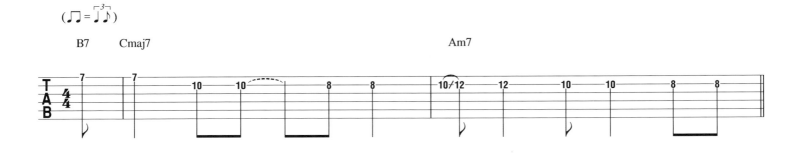

Arpeggios

Another great way to create ii–V–I licks is with arpeggios. This is especially helpful in getting the sound of the progression into your ear because you're playing nothing but chord tones.

Here's a very effective practice strategy: play eighth notes through the seventh chord arpeggio of each chord, and resolve to a nearby chord tone when changing chords. Obviously, you'll need to be familiar with some arpeggio fingerings for this to work, but even if you don't know a lot of them, this is a great way to expand your knowledge of the fretboard.

For example, over Dm7, we might play:

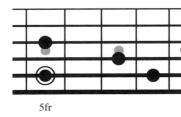

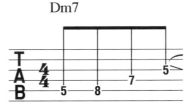

Now, the next chord is G7, so we want to resolve to a nearby chord tone of that chord—either G, B, D, or F. So, we have two choices nearby the last note we just played (C of the Dm7 chord): either the B on the fourth fret of the G string, or the D on the seventh fret of the G string. Let's resolve to the B and juggle the notes of G7 around a bit to get this.

From this final F note on the G7 chord to the change into the C chord, we could resolve to either the E note on the second fret of the D string or the G note on the fifth fret of the D string—we'll resolve to the E here. When you put the whole thing together, you'll get something like this:

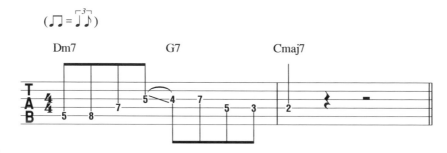

Try using this approach in different positions on the neck—it'll greatly expand your arpeggio vocabulary. You might come up with something like this:

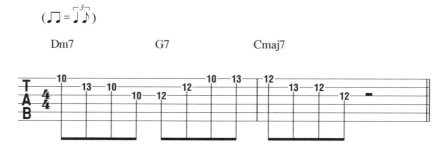

Be sure to study how the masters did it. Here's Johnny Smith's infamous three-octave Cmaj7 arpeggio (played starting on the 7th) from "Moonlight In Vermont." Reportedly, this lick had an influence on Pat Martino.

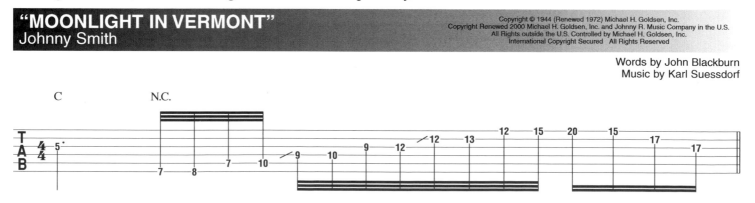

"MOONLIGHT IN VERMONT"
Johnny Smith

Words by John Blackburn
Music by Karl Suessdorf

This phrase from Tal Farlow's version on "I Remember You" emphasizes chord tones and features a nice arpeggio run in measure 3.

from the Paramount Picture THE FLEET'S IN
"I REMEMBER YOU"
Tal Farlow

Copyright © 1942 Sony/ATV Music Publishing LLC
Copyright Renewed
All Rights Administered by Sony/ATV Music Publishing LLC, 8 Music Square West, Nashville, TN 37203
International Copyright Secured   All Rights Reserved

Words by Johnny Mercer
Music by Victor Schertzinger

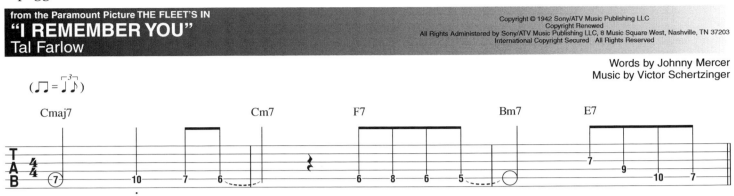

Extended Arpeggios

After you've gotten familiar with the seventh chord arpeggios, you can extend them to 9th chords to create more colorful sounds. You can get things like this.

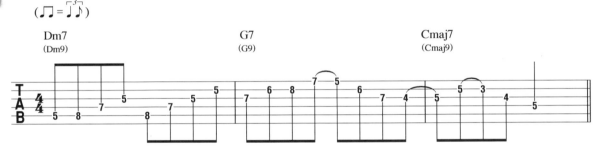

Notice that you don't have to run straight up or down each arpeggio; you can mix it up to get a more interesting melodic shape. As long as the chord tones are accounted for, have fun juggling the notes as you please. For example, check out the wide skips in the last measure of this lick.

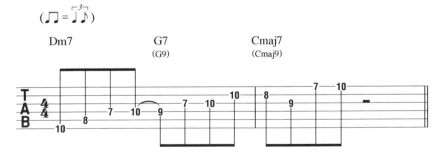

Later in Tal Farlow's "I Remember You" solo, he plays a neat, extended Cmaj9 arpeggio. Notice that the ii–V (Cm7–F7) in measure 2 resolves to the unusual Gmaj7, as opposed to the expected B♭.

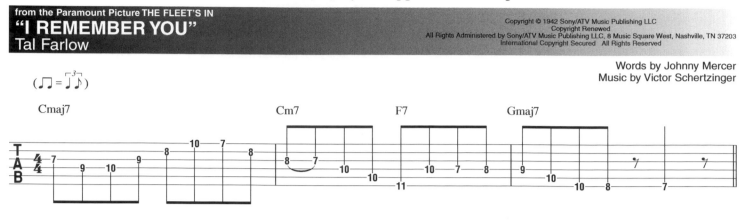

Words by Johnny Mercer
Music by Victor Schertzinger

Combining Scales and Arpeggios

The most commonly used method is usually a combination of scales and arpeggios—something like this, again from Tal Farlow's "I Remember You."

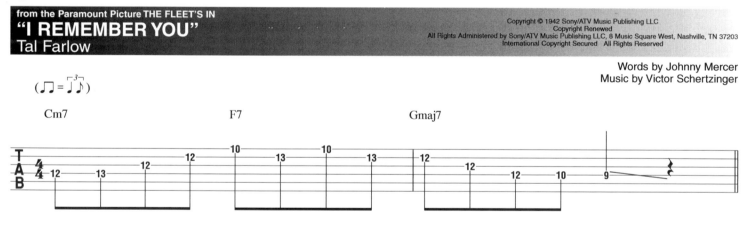

Words by Johnny Mercer
Music by Victor Schertzinger

We'll round out this lesson with a few examples using this technique. First, though, let's look at a few elements that most ii–V–I licks have in common.

1. **Chord tones on strong beats, passing tones on weak beats**

   Most licks will be arranged so that the stronger notes, the chord tones, will fall on the stronger beats, and the others, the passing tones, which can be from the scale or chromatic, will fall on the weaker beats.

2. **Stepwise resolution when changing chords**

   Licks will often move by step—meaning a whole step or a half step—as the progression moves to a new chord.

3. **Eighth-note rhythm**

   Many ii–V–I licks consist of nothing but eighth notes—at least through the ii and V chords.

   This isn't necessarily as important as the other two elements, because you'll often find triplets and sixteenth notes to mix things up in actual solos. The kind of notes you use also depends somewhat on the tempo; for fast tunes, continuous eighth notes are common, whereas for ballads or straight-eighth tunes, faster units like sixteenths are often employed. Playing all eighth notes, though, is an excellent way to practice.

Keep in mind that these are just guidelines, and in the real music world, things are hardly this tidy. But it's helpful in the beginning for solidifying the ii–V–I sound in your ear.

Now let's take a look at some licks that combine scales and arpeggios.

Here's one that uses a chromatic passing tone to resolve to the I chord.

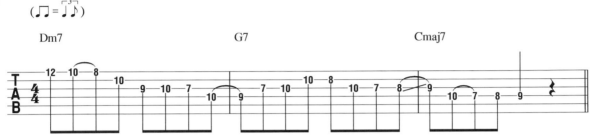

Let's try another one. This one will be in fifth position.

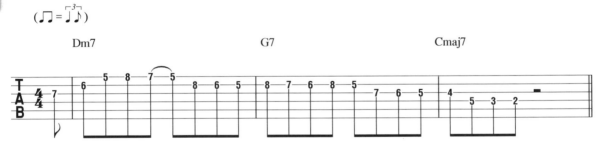

We've got two chromatic passing tones in that one, both over the G7 chord. Notice, though, that they're not offensive to the ear because they're placed on the upbeats and resolve to chord tones.

Here's another one. In this lick, we start off with a Dm9 arpeggio, but we lead into it with a chromatic pickup note. Then, we start to come down a G9 arpeggio and use a passing A♭ note to resolve to G, which is the 5th of the Cmaj7 chord. Then, over the C chord, we use notes from a Cmaj9 arpeggio with one passing F note to create a melody.

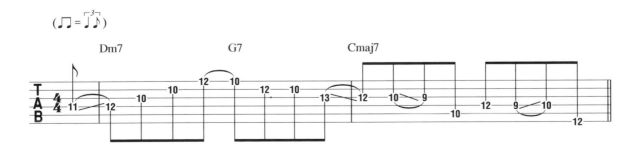

Here's Pat Martino burning through some ii–Vs in "Oleo."

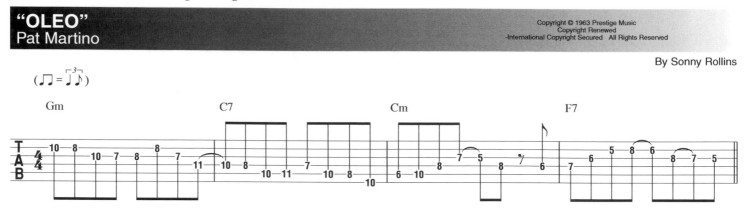

By Sonny Rollins

Remember to practice all of these ii–V–I ideas in all 12 twelve keys. Also, try actually writing out any new licks that you come up with so you don't forget them. Most licks can easily be turned into ten more by just varying one or two notes here and there. Before you know it, you'll have plenty to choose from when soloing.

JAZZ PHRASING

Jazz improvisation can be a confounding undertaking: you've got complex harmony, chord alterations, and shifting key centers, as well as a seemingly endless list of scales and modes from which to build your solos. On top of all that, once you choose the scale you're going to use, you've still got to phrase it properly to effectively tell your story.

Chord Tones

One of the keys to effective jazz phrasing is staying close to the chord tones, especially on the downbeat and when resolving notes. Doing this helps to give harmonic clarity to your lines. If you sound chord tones on the downbeat for most of the chords in a solo, the progression will be clear even *without* any accompaniment. Experienced jazzers would probably even be able to tell what song you were playing, if you really spelled out the changes in your lines.

 Let's try this over a C7–A7–D7–G7$\sharp$5 progression, which is a I–VI–II–V with functioning dominants, in the key of C. Note the placement of chord tones on the downbeats of each chord. Over the C chord, the first note played is G, the 5th. Over the A7 and D7 chords, the 3rds (C$\sharp$ and F$\sharp$, respectively) are sounded on the downbeats. When G7$\sharp$5 occurs, the first note played is the $\sharp$5 (D$\sharp$), and on the resolution to C, the 3rd (E) is sounded on the downbeat.

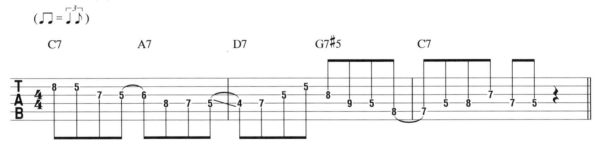

Here's an example of a line using only chord tones from the solo of "St. Thomas," played by Jim Hall. For the C chord, Hall hangs on to G, the 5th. Then over Dm7, he hits F, the $\flat$3rd, and then over the G7 chord, he hits G and F, the root and $\flat$7th, respectively, before resolving in measure 4 to E, the 3rd of C. Note this resolution E is anticipated, or played slightly earlier than the actual chord occurs. Anticipations are a vital technique of the jazz language and help keep phrases from becoming predictable or monotonous.

"ST. THOMAS"
Jim Hall

By Sonny Rollins

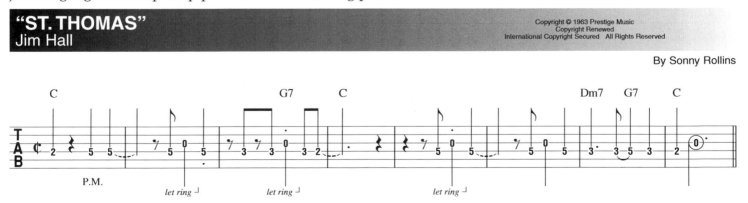

Here's another example from the same solo demonstrating the technique of using only chord tones. Note how Hall sometimes uses double stops here. While there aren't too many different notes played here, Hall's rhythmic phrasing keeps the line animated.

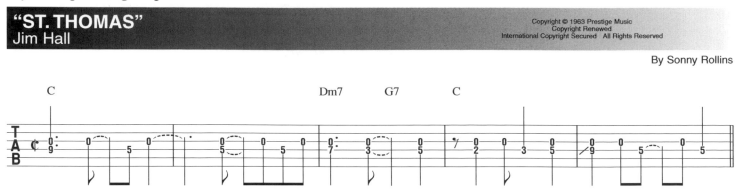

"ST. THOMAS"
Jim Hall

By Sonny Rollins

The cool thing about both of these Jim Hall examples is that while he is sticking only to chord tones, he's doing so in a highly musical way. Sometimes when jazz guitarists restrict themselves to only soloing with chord tones, they revert to running up and down arpeggios, which can sound mechanical, and at times, unmusical.

Now let's take a look at a standard ii–V–I lick, also in C. Again, this lick features strong chord tones on the downbeats of each chord change. On the downbeats of both the Dm7 chord and the Cmaj7 chord, the root (D and C, respectively) is sounded. Over the G7 chord, the 3rd (B) is sounded on the downbeat.

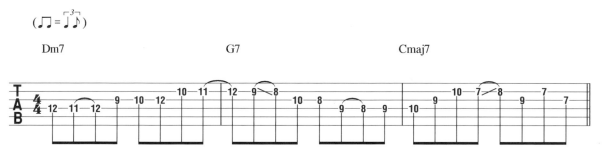

Chromaticism

While chord tones may be the most important tool for playing over chord changes, it's chromaticism that gives a jazz line that, well, "jazzy" flavor. Think about it like this, while Carlos Santana and Pat Martino both use the Dorian mode, Martino's use of chromaticism clearly marks him as a jazz player, whereas Santana is more of a "jazz-influenced" player.

Here's an example of a Pat Martino line from the bridge of "Oleo" that is riddled with chromatics. The chords here last for two measures each, so Martino really has time to add all of those chromatic notes. Check out how, regardless of how many chromatics are used, chord tones are still sounded at important moments. The first note over D7 is F♯, the 3rd. In measure 5, as soon as C7 arrives, the first note played is B♭, the ♭7th, and as soon as F7 occurs in measure 7, Martino hits the root. The placement of these chord tones is deliberate even amidst the speedy, long lines.

By Sonny Rollins

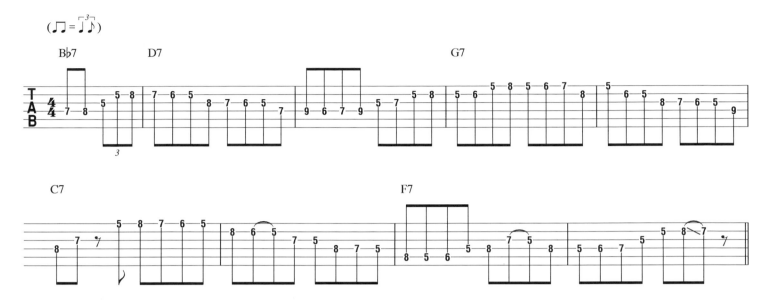

Passing Tones

Most often, chromatic notes appear in the guise of passing tones used to lead into a chord change. Passing tones add a hip, serpentine quality to jazz lines, while still maintaining a strong sense of tonality. When people think of jazz players and chromatics, they sometimes mistakenly think that the chromatic notes played are random—sometimes they are. In most cases however, the chromatics are carefully chosen to logically resolve to chord tones—even the craziest-sounding lines.

One of the things that passing tones allow you to do is construct longer phrases that flow seam-lessly from chord to chord. Here's a Tal Farlow–inspired line over a I–iii–VI–ii–V progression in C. Check out how the chromatic notes always resolve to chord tones—that's the crucial key to making them work!

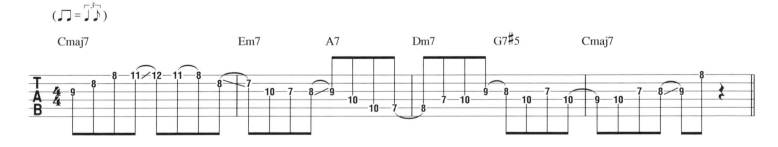

Here's Grant Green making use of passing tones. He fills in the holes chromatically from the 3rd, B to the 5th, D.

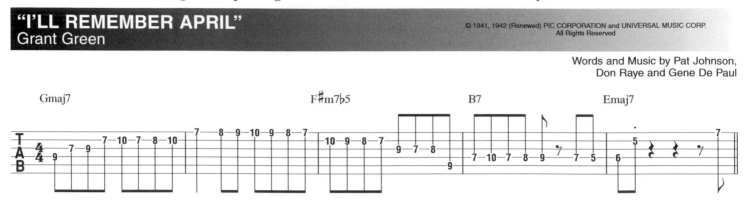

Here's a Pat Martino goodie from his solo on the John Coltrane classic, "Impressions." Note how the chromatic notes resolve by step.

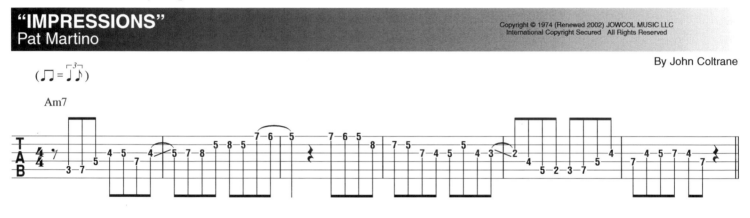

Charlie Parker Chromatics

Chromatics are also used to approach chord tones from a half step above or below. This was a favorite phrasing tool of the great bebop saxophonist, Charlie Parker. Here's a two-bar phrase using the half-step below approach over a D7 chord. Check out how F#, the 3rd, is approached by a half-step below on beat 2 of measure 1, and an octave higher in the next measure on the upbeat of beat 1.

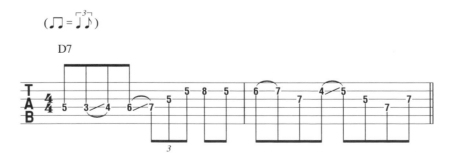

Here's an example of Grant Green making use of a Charlie Parker–influenced chromatic lick. In measure 2, the A on beat 1 is the 3rd of F7 and is the target note in this lick. Check out how it is encircled from above and below in the three notes that immediately precede it—the B♭ from above and the G and G♯ from below. This lick is a typical bop cliché and well worth committing to memory.

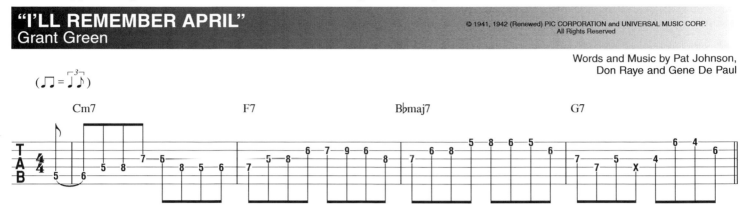

This particular pattern for encircling the 3rd from a half-step above and two consecutive half-steps below is among the most commonly heard of Charlie Parker licks and can be heard in the playing of virtually every jazzer that has roots in bebop.

In his solo on "On a Slow Boat to China," Barney Kessel uses this pattern frequently. In measure 2 over Gm7 to C7, E (3rd of C7) is targeted first from above F, then below, D–D♯. This figure occurs again over different chords in measure 4 (Am7 to D7). Here, F♯ (3rd of D7) is targeted from above by G, then below by F–F♯.

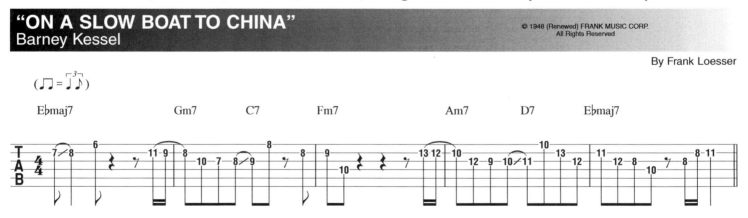

Here's Pat Metheny's take on the Parker lick. After resolving to Gmaj7, Metheny goes nuts with his slippery chromatic lines.

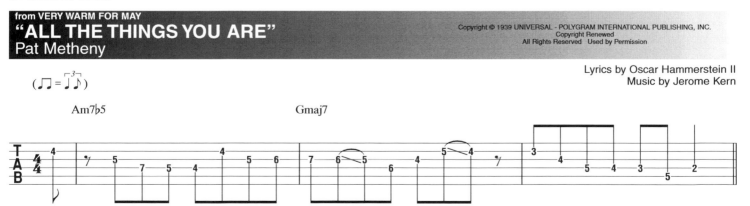

Chromatic Sequences

Another cool—and a little bit "outside"—way to use chromaticism is to take a motif and move it chromatically in and out of key. Chromatically moving a sequence around is pretty easy to do on guitar (just move the shape up or down a fret at a time) and can sound really cool. This kind of approach can be heard in the playing of more modern guitarists like Mike Stern and Pat Metheny.

Here's a four-note descending sequence in D Dorian, which is moved up and down the fretboard one fret at a time, over a static Dm11 chord. Note that the lines resolves perfectly to the root in measure 3. Again, the way to make any "outside" line work is by definitively resolving it.

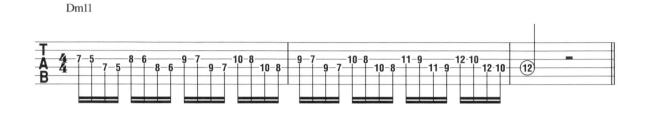

In this example over the tune "Solar," Pat Metheny takes this concept and really stretches it. The basic shape is a figure consisting of the pattern 5–3–2–1 played initially over C7 (against C7 the pattern is G–E–D–C). He moves this shape around—sometimes in half steps, sometimes in whole steps—and morphs it along the way, sometimes leaving notes out, sometimes starting the pattern on different beats, and sometimes changing the basic pattern (5–♭3–2–1 in measures 6–7 for example).

"SOLAR"
Pat Metheny

By Miles Davis

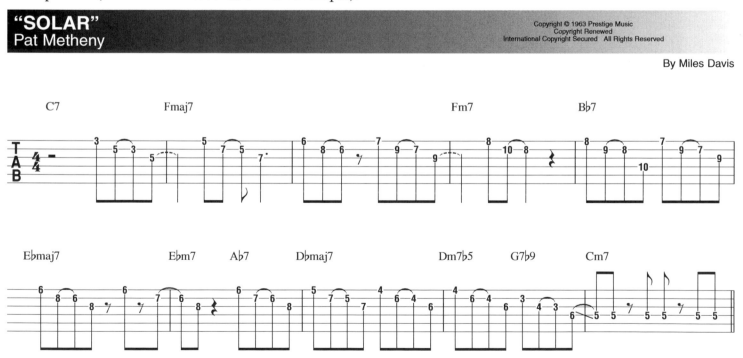

Forward-thinking bebopper, Joe Diorio, takes this approach and develops it into an ultra-hip passage in his solo on "Like Someone in Love."

"LIKE SOMEONE IN LOVE"

Words by Johnny Burke
Music by Jimmy Van Heusen

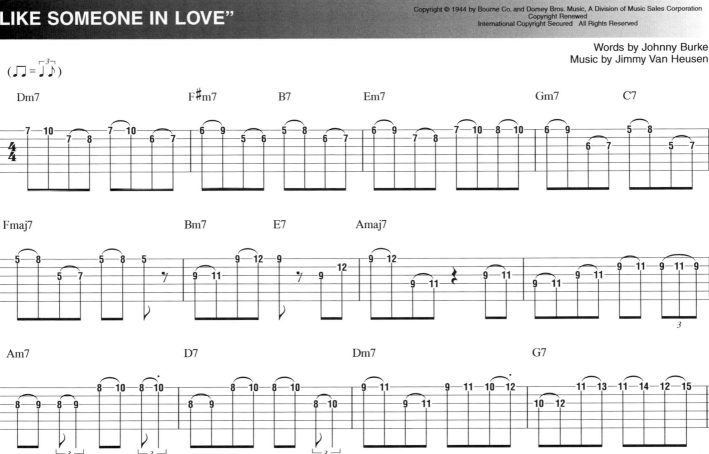

Got Blues?

Jazz guitarists often spend so much time dissecting melodic minor licks and diminished-scale runs, they forget about the good ol' blues scale. Many budding jazz guitarists try so hard to stick "hip" ideas into their playing, that they forget the most revered of jazz guitarists—giants like Wes Montgomery and George Benson—play blues scales almost as much as they play lightning-fast $13\flat9$ licks; and those guys are as good as jazz guitar gets!

Another cat who plays great bluesy, jazz lines is Kenny Burrell. Here's a Burell-esque line. Note that there are no string bends in this phrase, as is commonly found in the blues. Jazz guitarists generally frown upon string bending, probably because the older generation of jazz guitarists considered string bending "déclassé" because of its close ties to rock guitar. Instead, use slides and hammer-ons for a more horn-like sound and carefully work out the position shifts so your fingers won't get caught up.

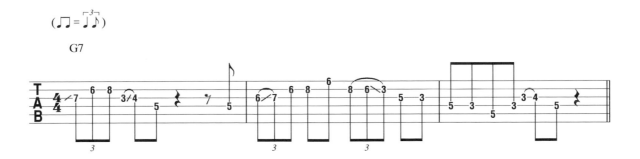

Here's how George Benson incorporates the blues scale into his jazz lines.

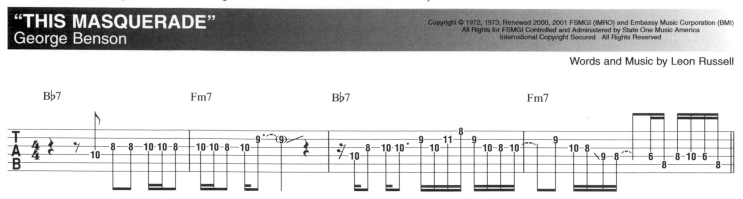

Words and Music by Leon Russell

Later in that same solo, Benson breaks the "rules" of jazz guitar by bending some notes.

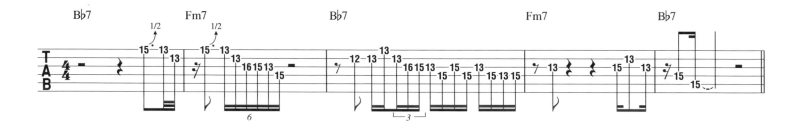

Octaves

If you find yourself repeatedly playing your "go-to" jazz licks and can't seem to break the cycle, try some octave phrases—they're a great way of adding another dimension to a solo.

Jazz guitar great Wes Montgomery was the undisputed champion of jazz octaves. His solos often had a three-tier approach with single-note lines followed by octaves and then chords. This gradual thickening of the texture really gave his solos a sense of unstoppable momentum. Here's a four-bar phrase typical of Montgomery's octave technique. Use your pick-hand's thumb to strike the strings, and mute the other strings with your left hand to keep the octaves clean.

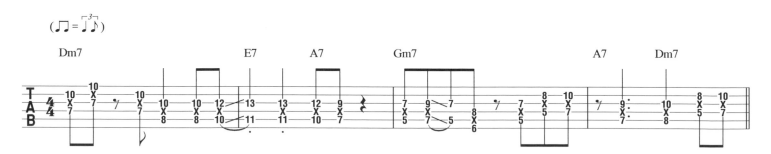

A good way to practice octaves is to learn jazz "heads" in octaves. Here's Wes shakin' things up on the head out to "Yesterdays."

"YESTERDAYS"
Wes Montgomery

Words by Otto Harbach
Music by Jerome Kern

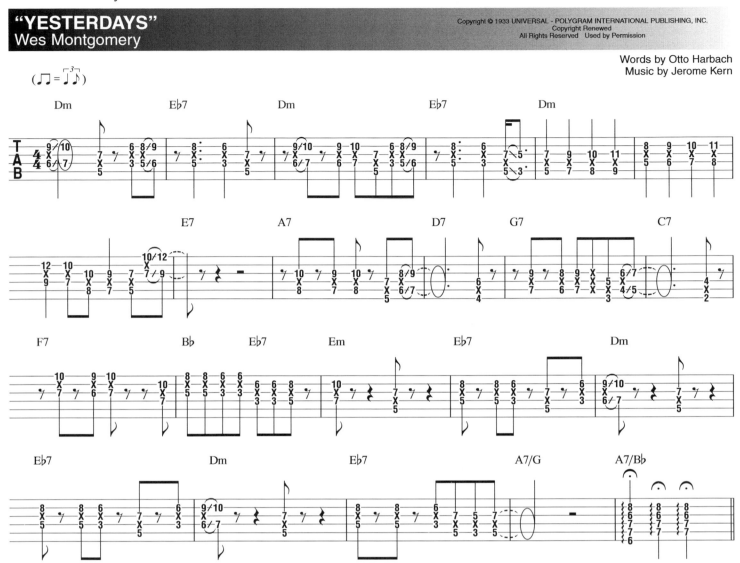

Here's Joe Pass capping off a single-note run with octaves.

"YARDBIRD SUITE"
Joe Pass

By Charlie Parker

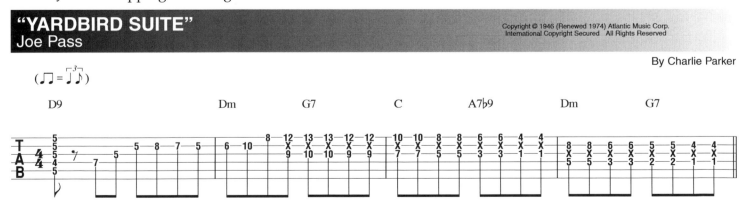

Triad Superimposition

Occasionally, you'll come across a song with static harmony. Though at first you might be relieved that there are no changes to navigate, you might also be stuck thinking "okay, how do I make this solo interesting with only one chord?" In these cases, it might be in your best interest to pretend as if there were chord changes. One way to do this is to use triad superimposition. Here's how it works.

Let's say you're presented with a static G7 harmony for four bars. Instead of thinking G Mixolydian (G–A–B–C–D–E–F), you could instead simply choose two triads from the G Mixolydian mode, say, F and G, and use the notes from those two chords to build your phrase, like this. Although these notes are found in the G Mixolydian mode, the deliberate emphasis of these notes and the omission of other notes in the mode present a nice, open sound.

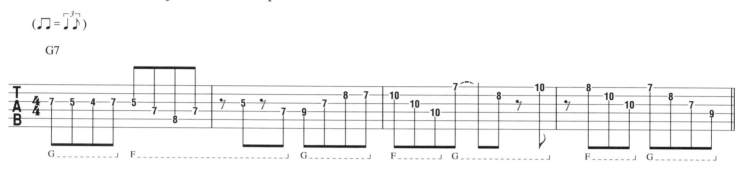

Here, Pat Metheny takes the two aforementioned triads, F and G, and plays them over Fmaj7. The G triad against Fmaj7 yields the colorful 9th (G), ♯11th (B), and 13th (D).

"SOLAR"
Pat Metheny

By Miles Davis

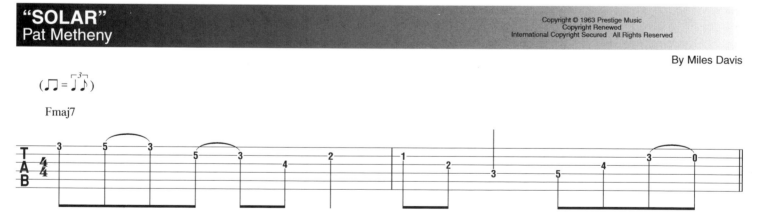

Out Sounds

 You can also use triad superimposition to create "outside" sounds, by choosing two triads that contain altered tones of the harmony chord. This is a favorite phrasing tool of guitarist Mike Stern, who picked up this type of idea from his mentor, jazz guru, pianist Charlie Banacos. Here's a Stern-style "outside" line drawing from E and E♭ triads over G7.

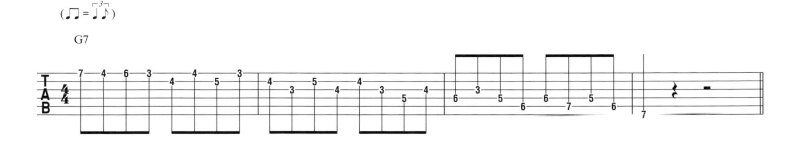

Earlier we saw Pat Metheny using triads in his solo on "Solar." Here, from that same solo, he gets a little wilder over the same Fmaj7 chord. He takes two augmented triads (C+ and D+) and superimposes them to create a Michael Brecker/Walt Weiskopf-inspired "out" line. This is noticeably different from the other example, because whereas the superimposed F and G triads in the earlier example resulted in colorful yet commonplace notes, some of the tensions created from the triads in this lick—♭9 (F♯, G♭ enharmonically) and ♯9 (G♯)—are not normally used on maj7 chords (at least not in a mainstream jazz context).

"SOLAR"
Pat Metheny

By Miles Davis

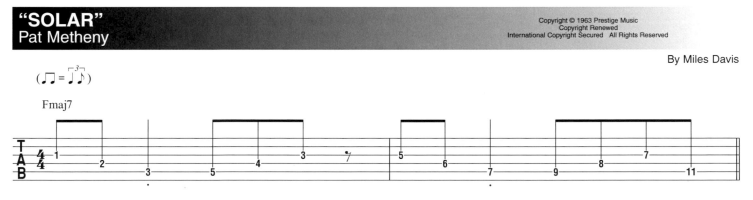

In his solo over "That's What You Think," Stern superimposes a G♭ triad (measure 1 beats 3–4) and a D♭ triad (measure 2 beats 3–4) over F7.

"THAT'S WHAT YOU THINK"
Mike Stern

By Mike Stern

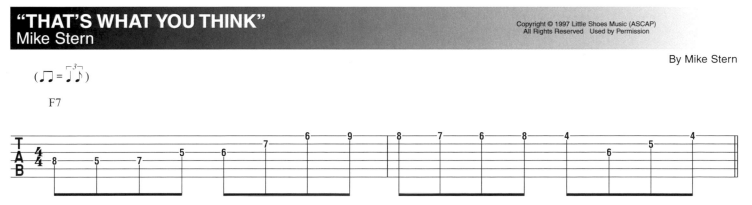

Grant Green plays a D♭ augmented triad over Cm7 and moves the augmented triad up in whole steps (E♭+–F+–G+–A+) taking a nice harmonic detour. These triads are derived from the D♭ whole tone scale (D♭–E♭–F–G–A–B).

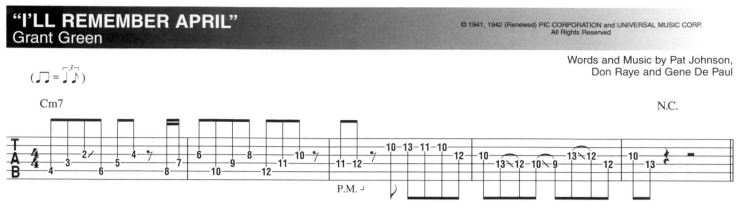

Words and Music by Pat Johnson,
Don Raye and Gene De Paul

Implied Coltrane Changes

Another superimposition approach over a static harmony is to use chord tones to imply well-known chord progressions, like Coltrane changes.

 This phrase superimposes the changes of Coltrane's "Countdown" over a static Cm7 chord. Even though the line zig-zags through a lot of chords, its final resolution keeps everything intact. Fasten your seatbelts and come on for the ride!

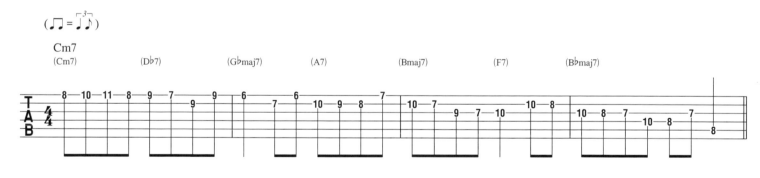

Quotation

The final phrasing tool we're going to cover is the ever-popular art of quotation. This is an especially effective phrasing approach, as it tends to really grab the audience's attention, even if they don't understand anything else that's been played all night. For example, sometimes in his live shows, Mike Stern may quote Jimi Hendrix's "Third Stone From the Sun" or even "Smoke on the Water."

Here's a ii–V–I phrase with a quote from Thelonious Monk's "Straight, No Chaser" over the V chord.

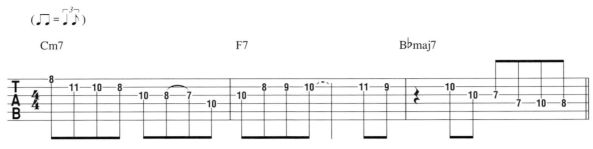

In his "Impressions" solo, Pat Martino sticks in a quote from Rimsky-Korsakov's "Flight of the Bumblebee." This is a commonly used quote for virtuosic solos; learn it and try sticking it in next time you're taking a burning solo.

"IMPRESSIONS"
Pat Martino

By John Coltrane

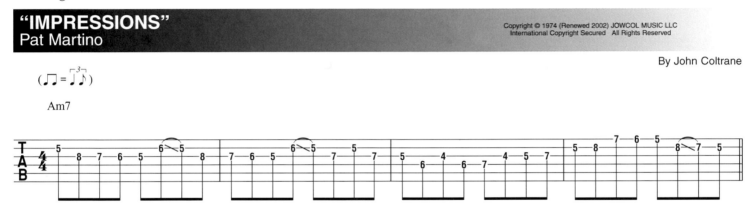

IMPROVE YOUR IMPROV
AND OTHER JAZZ TECHNIQUES WITH BOOKS FROM HAL LEONARD

JAZZ GUITAR
Hal Leonard Guitar Method
by Jeff Schroedl

The Hal Leonard Jazz Guitar Method is your complete guide to learning jazz guitar. This book uses real jazz songs to teach the basics of accompanying and improvising jazz guitar in the style of Wes Montgomery, Joe Pass, Tal Farlow, Charlie Christian, Pat Martino, Barney Kessel, Jim Hall, and many others.
00695359 Book/Online Audio $19.99

AMAZING PHRASING
50 Ways to Improve Your
Improvisational Skills • *by Tom Kolb*

This book explores all the main components necessary for crafting well-balanced rhythmic and melodic phrases. It also explains how these phrases are put together to form cohesive solos. Many styles are covered – rock, blues, jazz, fusion, country, Latin, funk and more – and all of the concepts are backed up with musical examples.
00695583 Book/Online Audio $19.99

BEST OF JAZZ GUITAR
by Wolf Marshall • Signature Licks

In this book/CD pack, Wolf Marshall provides a hands-on analysis of 10 of the most frequently played tunes in the jazz genre, as played by the leading guitarists of all time. Each selection includes technical analysis and performance notes, biographical sketches, and authentic matching audio with backing tracks.
00695586 Book/CD Pack... $24.95

CHORD-MELODY PHRASES FOR GUITAR
by Ron Eschete • REH ProLessons Series

Expand your chord-melody chops with these outstanding jazz phrases! This book covers: chord substitutions, chromatic movements, contrary motion, pedal tones, inner-voice movements, reharmonization techniques, and much more. Includes standard notation and tab, and a CD.
00695628 Book/CD Pack... $17.99

CHORDS FOR JAZZ GUITAR
The Complete Guide to Comping,
Chord Melody and Chord Soloing • *by Charlton Johnson*

This book/audio pack will teach you how to play jazz chords all over the fretboard in a variety of styles and progressions. It covers: voicings, progressions, jazz chord theory, comping, chord melody, chord soloing, voice leading and many more topics. The audio offers 98 full-band demo tracks. No tablature.
00695706 Book/Online Audio $19.95

FRETBOARD ROADMAPS – JAZZ GUITAR
The Essential Guitar Patterns
That All the Pros Know and Use • *by Fred Sokolow*

This book will get guitarists playing lead & rhythm anywhere on the fretboard, in any key! It teaches a variety of lead guitar styles using moveable patterns, double-note licks, sliding pentatonics and more, through easy-to-follow diagrams and instructions. The online audio includes 54 full-demo tracks.
00695354 Book/Online Audio $15.99

JAZZ IMPROVISATION FOR GUITAR
by Les Wise • REH ProLessons Series

This book/audio will allow you to make the transition from playing disjointed scales and arpeggios to playing melodic jazz solos that maintain continuity and interest for the listener. Topics covered include: tension and resolution, major scale, melodic minor scale, and harmonic minor scale patterns, common licks and substitution techniques, creating altered tension, and more! Features standard notation and tab, and online audio.
00695657 Book/Online Audio $17.99

JAZZ RHYTHM GUITAR
The Complete Guide
by Jack Grassel

This book/CD pack will help rhythm guitarists better understand: chord symbols and voicings, comping styles and patterns, equipment, accessories and set-up, the fingerboard, chord theory, and much more. The accompanying CD includes 74 full-band tracks.
00695654 Book/CD Pack... $19.95

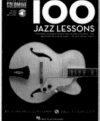

JAZZ SOLOS FOR GUITAR
Lead Guitar in the Styles of Tal Farlow,
Barney Kessel, Wes Montgomery, Joe Pass, Johnny Smith
by Les Wise

Examine the solo concepts of the masters with this book including phrase-by-phrase performance notes, tips on arpeggio substitution, scale substitution, tension and resolution, jazz-blues, chord soloing, and more. The audio includes full demonstration and rhythm-only tracks.
00695447 Book/Online Audio $19.99

100 JAZZ LESSONS
Guitar Lesson Goldmine Series
by John Heussenstamm and Paul Silbergleit

Featuring 100 individual modules covering a giant array of topics, each lesson includes detailed instruction with playing examples presented in standard notation and tablature. You'll also get extremely useful tips, scale diagrams, and more to reinforce your learning experience, plus audio featuring performance demos of all the examples in the book!
00696454 Book/Online Audio $24.99

101 MUST-KNOW JAZZ LICKS
A Quick, Easy Reference Guide
for All Guitarists • *by Wolf Marshall*

Here are 101 definitive licks, plus demonstration audio, from every major jazz guitar style, neatly organized into easy-to-use categories. They're all here: swing and pre-bop, bebop, post-bop modern jazz, hard bop and cool jazz, modal jazz, soul jazz and postmodern jazz. Includes an introduction, tips, and a list of suggested recordings.
00695433 Book/Online Audio $17.99

SWING AND BIG BAND GUITAR
Four-to-the-Bar Comping in the Style of
Freddie Green • *by Charlton Johnson*

This unique package teaches the essentials of swing and big band styles, including chord voicings, inversions, substitutions; time and groove, reading charts, chord reduction, and expansion; sample songs, patterns, progressions, and exercises; chord reference library; and online audio with over 50 full-demo examples. Uses chord grids – no tablature.
00695147 Book/Online Audio $19.99

HAL•LEONARD®
Visit Hal Leonard Online at **www.halleonard.com**

Prices, contents and availability
subject to change without notice.